How To Cook Vegetarian Food

The Secrets For 50 Delicious Recipes With Just 5 Inredients

Brigitte S. Romeo

How To Cook Vegetarian Food

© Copyright 2021 - All rights reserved.

The content contained within this book may not be reproduced, duplicated or transmitted without direct written permission from the author or the publisher.

Under no circumstances will any blame or legal responsibility be held against the publisher, or author, for any damages, reparation, or monetary loss due to the information contained within this book. Either directly or indirectly.

Legal Notice:

This book is copyright protected. This book is only for personal use. You cannot amend, distribute, sell, use, quote or paraphrase any part, or the content within this book, without the consent of the author or publisher.

Disclaimer Notice:

Please note the information contained within this document is for educational and entertainment purposes only. All effort has been executed to present accurate, up to date, and reliable, complete information. No warranties of any kind are declared or implied. Readers acknowledge that the author is not engaging in the rendering of legal, financial, medical or professional advice. The content within this book has been derived from various sources. Please consult a licensed professional before attempting any techniques outlined in this book.

By reading this document, the reader agrees that under no circumstances is the author responsible for any losses, direct or indirect, which are incurred as a result of the use of information contained within this document, including, but not limited to, errors, omissions, or inaccuracies.

TABLE OF CONTENTS

INTRODUCTION **8**

CHAPTER 1: BREAKFAST RECIPES **12**

1. MINI FRITTATAS 12
2. BREAKFAST HASH 14
3. SWISS CHARD MUFFIN 16
4. NUTMEG BANANA QUINOA 18
5. CABBAGE SOUP 20
6. LIME GINGER GREEN BEANS 21
7. GARLIC SPINACH 23
8. GREEN CURRY MUSHROOMS 25

CHAPTER 2: LUNCH RECIPES **28**

9. JAPANESE SUSHI RICE 28
10. LEMON MOZZARELLA PASTA 30
11. ZUCCHINI NOODLES 32
12. MASHED POTATOES AND KALE WITH WHITE BEANS 33

CHAPTER 3: MAIN MEALS RECIPES **36**

13. SPAGHETTI BOLOGNESE 36
14. BLACK BEAN QUINOA BURGERS 38
15. TOMATO CURRY FRITTERS 40

CHAPTER 4: VEGETABLES, SALADS AND SIDES RECIPES **42**

16. STRAWBERRY BLUE CHEESE ARUGULA SALAD 42
17. CUCUMBER HUMMUS WRAPS 44
18. WHITE BEAN SALAD 46
19. QUICK WHITE BEAN SALAD 48
20. EASY GREEN BEAN SALAD 50

21.	SUPERCHARGING AVOCADO CHICKPEA SALAD	52
22.	WATERMELON SALAD	54
23.	VEGETABLE FRIED BROWN RICE	56

CHAPTER 5: DESSERT RECIPES 58

24.	CHOCOLATE-PEPPERMINT NICE CREAM	58
25.	STRAWBERRY-WATERMELON ICE POPS	60
26.	OAT CRUNCH APPLE CRISP	61

CHAPTER 6: SNACK RECIPES 64

27.	TERIYAKI TEMPEH AND BROCCOLI	65
28.	PEACH CRISP	67
29.	BANANA BREAD	69
30.	MEXICAN BEANS AND RICE	71
31.	SPAGHETTI SQUASH WITH FETA	73
32.	ZUCCHINI NOODLES WITH MARINARA SAUCE	75
33.	COCONUT CURRY WITH VEGETABLES	77

CHAPTER 7: JUICES AND SMOOTHIES RECIPES 80

34.	ENDLESS ENERGY SMOOTHIE	80
35.	HIGH-FIBRE FRUIT SMOOTHIE	82
36.	NUTRITIOUS GREEN SMOOTHIE	83
37.	APRICOT, STRAWBERRY, AND BANANA SMOOTHIE	84
38.	SPINACH AND GREEN APPLE SMOOTHIE	85
39.	SUPER FOOD BLUEBERRY SMOOTHIE	86

CHAPTER 8: OTHER RECIPES 88

40.	SQUASH LENTIL SOUP	89
41.	SWEET POTATO GNOCCHI	91
42.	TACO PASTA BOWL	94
43.	VEGAN BBQ TOFU	96

44.	Mustard Tomato Mix	98
45.	Veggies and noodle bowl with mushrooms	99
46.	Broccoli over Orzo	100
47.	Mango Pineapple Hoisin Sauce	102
48.	Sriracha Sauce	103
49.	White Sauce (Béchamel)	105
50.	Butter Bean Hummus	107

CONCLUSION **108**

INTRODUCTION

What does it mean to be a vegetarian?

A Vegetarian is a person who does not eat meat, poultry, or fish. Vegetarians eat only plant foods such as fruits, vegetables, legumes, and grains or products made from them. Some people think of a vegetarian as a person who does not eat red meat but may consume fish and chicken. Other people consider a vegetarian to be someone who avoids eating all animal flesh, including fish, poultry, and red meat. However, "true" vegetarians avoid the consumption of all meats, including fish and chicken.

Vegetarianism is not a new concept; it has been practiced since ancient times in India during the Vedic period (1500-500 BC) as well as in Greece and Rome. It continues to be practiced today in modern society around the world. In most cases, it is a matter of individual choice.

Eating meat and fish has been a common practice all over the world for thousands of years. In some cultures, the preparation of the meat or fish symbolizes wealth and luxury, while in others it represents a source of survival. Today, people are becoming more aware of the impact that their food choices have on their health as well as on the environment.

So, specifically, what are the foods that one needs to avoid? These are as follows:

- Beef
- Pork
- Lamb
- Veal
- All Game (deer, elk, etc.)
- Any other land mammal that's been fed animal products or by-products such as eggs and dairy (many land mammals are herbivores)
- Fish and Shellfish
- Goose and Duck
- Emu and Alligator
- Any other animal that is not a seafood product
- Animal by-products such as gelatin (e.g., gummy bears)

As a vegetarian, what specific foods do you avoid? For starters, you can limit your consumption of the following:

- Pork and bacon
- Eggs (or eat only eggs that are certified organic or non-cage free)

- Dairy products (or consume only dairy products that are certified organic)

- All products that are made from animals, such as leather shoes, belts, jackets, etc.

What are the substitutes that you use to replace the meat and fish that you avoid?

- Tofu (made from soybeans)

- Tempeh (made from soybeans)

- TVP (textured vegetable protein)

- Seitan (very high in protein, available as steak strips or chicken-style pieces)

- Soy Nuggets/Sausage

Being a vegetarian has its benefits, but there are definitely some challenges as well. If you are considering the option of being a vegetarian, the most important thing to consider is your overall health. However, if you have concerns with the lack of protein in your diet, believe that it's unwise to eat only plant products, or simply crave meat and fish and think you can't give them up without feeling hungry or deprived, then the choice of becoming a vegetarian may not be the right one for you.

This vegetarian cookbook will help you get a delicious and healthy recipe on the table that will make your life less stressful. A good recipe doesn't need a long list of ingredients to make it tasty, and while preparing meals may seem hard. You can eat together a healthy family food in the same amount of time you'd need to order takeout!

This vegetarian cookbook will show you a variety of dishes you can make with easy-to-find ingredients. This is the perfect practical guide for anyone looking to make a variety of delicious meals that are healthy. It includes recipes for breakfast, lunch, dinner, appetizers, and desserts, as well as those for snacks and sides. Whether looking to lose weight or just eat more healthily, this cookbook will make it easier than ever before!

So, let us begin the journey.

CHAPTER 1:

BREAKFAST RECIPES

1. Mini Frittatas

Preparation Time: 5 minutes

Cooking Time: 5 minutes

Servings: 2

Ingredients:

- 3 eggs
- ½ cup coconut milk
- ½ teaspoon salt and pepper
- ¼ cup kale
- ¼ cup chopped broccoli
- 1 cup of water

Directions:

1. Mix eggs, milk, kale, broccoli, salt, and pepper and mix in a dish.

2. Pour mixture into individual baking molds using silicone molds.

3. Place molds on a rack in Instant Pot with 1 cup of water.

4. Set Instant Pot to Manual and High Pressure for 5 minutes.

5. When the timer goes off, and cooking is done, perform a quick steam release.

6. Enjoy!

Nutrition: Calories 242 Fat 20.9g Saturated Fat 14.7g Cholesterol 246mg Carbohydrate 5.8g Fiber 1.9g

2. Breakfast Hash

Preparation Time: 5 minutes

Cooking Time: 5 minutes

Servings: 2

Ingredients:

- 1 tablespoon coconut oil
- 2 small sweet potatoes, peeled if desired
- 2 eggs
- 1/4 cup water
- 1 cup shredded parmesan cheese

Directions:

1. Set the Instant Pot to "Sauté" and add a thin layer of coconut oil to the bottom of the pan. While the Instant Pot is heating, finely shred the sweet potatoes in a food processor. Squeeze out any excess moisture, then add the shredded sweet potatoes to the hot oil. Let the sweet potatoes brown in the hot oil without stirring.

2. Meanwhile, beat the eggs and set them aside.

3. Once the sweet potatoes have browned on the bottom, break them up with a wooden spoon. Add the water, eggs, parmesan cheese, stir gently.

4. Lock the cover on the Instant Pot and bring it to High Pressure. Let cook for 1 minute and then use the Quick-release method to release the steam.

5. Serve the breakfast hash immediately.

Nutrition: Calories 344 Fat 14.4g Cholesterol 174mg Carbohydrate 42.7g Fiber 6.2g

3. **Swiss Chard Muffin**

Preparation Time: 5 minutes

Cooking Time: 10 minutes

Servings: 2

Ingredients:

- 2 eggs
- 1/8 teaspoon pepper seasoning
- 4 tablespoons shredded goat cheese
- 1 green onion, diced
- ½ cup Swiss chard chopped
- 1 1/2 cups water

Directions:

1. Put the steamer basket in the Instant Pot and add 1 1/2 cups water.

2. Break eggs into a large measuring bowl with pour spout, add pepper, and beat well. Divide the cheese, Swiss chard, and green

onion evenly between silicone muffin cups. Pour the beaten eggs into each muffin cup and stir with a fork to combine.

3. Place muffin cups on a steamer basket. Cover and lock lid in place. Select High Pressure and 8 minutes cook time. When the timer beeps, turn off, wait two minutes, then use a quick pressure release.

4. Carefully open the lid, lift out the steamer basket, and remove muffin cups.

5. Serve immediately.

Nutrition: Calories 66 Fat 4.7g Cholesterol 89mg Carbohydrate 0.8g Fiber 0.2g

4. Nutmeg Banana Quinoa

Preparation Time: 10 minutes

Cooking Time: 5 minutes

Servings: 2

Ingredients:

- 1 cup quinoa
- 1 cup soy milk
- 1 cup of water
- 2 bananas
- 1 teaspoon nutmeg
- 1 tablespoon honey

Directions:

1. Add in the quinoa, soy milk, and water in Instant Pot.
2. Slice up 1 of the bananas and add it into the Instant Pot. Add in nutmeg and honey. Stir.
3. Set the Manual button to 5 minutes. Once the timer beeps, let the pressure release naturally for 10 minutes and then carefully

release the rest of the pressure. Be careful, though, since grains can really get foamy.

4. Stir the quinoa and scoop into bowls. Slice the second banana and add fresh slices to the top of each bowl.

Nutrition: Calories 522 Fat 8.1g Cholesterol 0mg Carbohydrate 98.4g Fiber 10g

5. Cabbage Soup

Preparation Time: 10 minutes

Cooking Time: 20 minutes

Servings: 2

Ingredients:

- 1 head cabbage
- ½ tablespoon dried basil
- 2 oz Cheddar cheese chunks
- ½ tablespoon coconut cream
- ½ teaspoon garlic powder
- Salt to taste

Directions:

1. Add all ingredients to the blender pitcher and lock the lid.
2. Select the "Soup" setting for 20 minutes.
3. Garnish with shredded cheddar cheese and serve.

Nutrition: Calories 213 Fat 10.5g Cholesterol 29mg Carbohydrate 21.8g Fiber 9.1g

6. Lime Ginger Green Beans

Preparation Time: 5 minutes

Cooking Time: 15 minutes

Servings: 2

Ingredients:

- 2 cups green beans, cut into 4 inches
- 1 cup water
- 1 tablespoon vegetable oil
- 2 teaspoons freshly squeezed lime juice
- ½ teaspoon salt
- 1 teaspoon ginger powder

Directions:

1. Place the green beans in a steamer basket and put the basket into the Instant Pot. Add the water. Lock the lid and turn the steam release handle to sealing. Using the Manual or Pressure Cook function, set the cooker to Low Pressure for 15 minutes.

2. When the cooking time is complete, quickly release the pressure.

3. In a serving bowl, stir together the vegetable oil, lime juice, salt, and ginger powder.

4. Carefully remove the lid and add the green beans to the bowl. Toss to combine. Taste and add the remaining lemon juice or ginger as needed.

Nutrition: Calories 121 Fat 7g Cholesterol 0mg Carbohydrate 12.2g Fiber 4.1g

7. Garlic Spinach

Preparation Time: 5 minutes

Cooking Time: 5 minutes

Servings: 2

Ingredients:

- ½ tablespoon unsalted butter
- 1 tablespoon garlic powder
- 2 cups fresh spinach
- ¼ teaspoon salt
- ½ lemon, juiced

Directions:

1. Select Sauté on the Instant Pot. When the pot is hot, add butter.
2. Stir in the garlic powder; cook and stir until the garlic is fragrant, about 30 seconds.
3. Add the spinach a few handfuls at a time, secure the lid on the pot.

4. Close the pressure-release valve. Select Manual and set the pot at High Pressure for 5 minutes.

5. At the end of the cooking time, allow the pot to sit undisturbed for 10 minutes, then release any remaining pressure, stir in the lemon juice, and season with salt.

Nutrition: Calories 51 Fat 3.1g Cholesterol 8mg Carbohydrate 5.5g Fiber 1.5g

8. Green Curry Mushrooms

Preparation Time: 15 minutes

Cooking Time: 10 minutes

Servings: 2

Ingredients:

- 1 ½ cups water
- 1 1/2 tablespoons vegetable oil
- 1 cup mushrooms, drained and cubed
- ¼ teaspoon salt
- 1 cup soy milk
- 1 tablespoon green curry paste

Directions:

1. Select Sauté on the Instant Pot. When the Instant Pot is hot, add vegetable oil. Stir in mushrooms. Stirring occasionally, fry about 5 minutes, until evenly crisp and lightly browned. Season with salt.

2. Add soy milk green curry paste.

3. Secure the lid on the pot. Close the pressure-release valve. Select Manual and set the pot at High Pressure for 5 minutes. At the end of the cooking time, allow the pot to sit undisturbed for 10 minutes, then release any remaining pressure.

Nutrition: Calories 237 Fat 15.7g Cholesterol 0mg Carbohydrate 12.1g Fiber 1.9g

CHAPTER 2:

LUNCH RECIPES

9. Japanese Sushi Rice

Preparation Time: 5 minutes

Cooking Time: 20 minutes

Servings: 2

Ingredients:

- 2 cups water
- 1 teaspoon salt
- 1 teaspoon honey
- ½ sheet nori
- 1 cup uncooked white rice (sushi rice)

Directions:

1. In an Instant Pot, combine the water, salt, honey, and nori. Bring to a boil and add the rice.

2. Close the pressure-release valve. Select Manual and set the pot at High Pressure for 10 minutes. At the end of the cooking time, allow the pot to sit undisturbed for 10 minutes, then release any remaining pressure.

3. Serve and enjoy.

Nutrition: Calories 340 Fat 0.6g Cholesterol 0mg Carbohydrate 76.8g Fiber 1.5g

10. Lemon Mozzarella Pasta

Preparation Time: 5 minutes

Cooking Time: 10 minutes

Servings: 2

Ingredients:

- 4 oz. macaroni
- ¼ cup peas
- ½ cup mozzarella cheese
- ½ tablespoon olive oil
- 1 lemon
- Salt and pepper

Directions:

1. Set Instant Pot to Sauté. Add the olive oil and allow it to sizzle. Add macaroni, peas, lemon, salt, and pepper.

2. Lock lid. Set pressure cook on high pressure for 10 minutes. When cooking time ends, release pressure and wait for steam to completely stop before opening the lid.

3. Add mozzarella cheese and Stir until everything is combined and coated with sauce.

4. Enjoy.

Nutrition: Calories 273 Fat 5.9g Carbohydrate 46.6g Protein 10.3g

11. Zucchini Noodles

Preparation Time: 10 minutes Cooking Time: 15 minutes

Servings: 2

Ingredients:

- 2 zucchini, peeled
- Marinara sauce of your choice
- Any other seasonings you wish to use

Directions:

1. Peel & spiralizer your zucchini into noodles.
2. Add some of your favorite sauce to Instant Pot, hit "Sauté" and "Adjust," so it's on the "More" or "High" setting.
3. Once the sauce is boiling, add now the noodles to the pot. Toss the noodles in the sauce and allow them to heat up and soften for a few minutes for about 2-5 minutes.
4. Serve in the bowls and top with grated parmesan, if desired.

Nutrition: Calories 86 Fat 2g Cholesterol 1mg Carbohydrate 15.2g Fiber 3.8g

12. Mashed Potatoes and Kale with White Beans

Preparation Time: 10 minutes

Cooking Time: 30 minutes

Servings: 4

Ingredients:

- 2 large Russet potatoes
- Pinch salt (optional), plus ½ teaspoon
- ½ cup vegetable broth
- 6 ounces kale, torn into bite-size pieces
- 1 (14.5-ounce) can great northern beans or other white beans, rinsed and drained
- ¼ to ½ teaspoon freshly ground black pepper, to taste

Directions:

1. Wash (but don't peel!) the potatoes, quarter them, then halve each quarter. Place in a large pot and cover with water. Add a pinch of salt (if using) and bring to a boil. Cover, reduce the heat

to medium, and cook for about 20 minutes until the potatoes are tender.

2. Drain the potatoes and return to the pot. Pour the vegetable broth over the potatoes. Add the kale and then the beans. Cover and cook on low heat for about 5 minutes, until the kale turns bright green and is lightly wilted.

3. Use a potato masher to mash everything together, and season with ½ teaspoon salt and pepper.

4. Divide the potatoes, kale, and beans evenly among 4 single-serving containers. Let cool before sealing the lids.

Nutrition: Calories: 255 Total fat: 1g Carbohydrates: 53g Fiber: 11g

CHAPTER 3:

MAIN MEALS RECIPES

13. Spaghetti Bolognese

Preparation Time: 15 minutes

Cooking Time: 5 minutes

Servings: 4

Ingredients:

- 2 cups Whole wheat spaghetti (dry)
- 1 7-ounces pack textured soy mince
- 3 cloves Garlic (minced)
- 1 cup Tomato cubes (canned or fresh)
- ¼ cup Basil (fresh or dried)

Directions:

1. Cook spaghetti according to instructions of its package, drain the water with a strainer, then set it aside.

2. Put a non-stick deep frying pan over medium-high heat and add the soy mince, minced garlic, tomato cubes, and basil.

3. Cook it for about 2 minutes and stir occasionally until everything is cooked.

4. Turn off the heat, the divide the spaghetti between 2 plates, and add half of the sauce on top of the spaghetti on each plate.

5. Serve with the optional toppings and enjoy!

6. Store the spaghetti and sauce in an airtight container in the fridge.

7. You can consume this within 3 days. Also, it can be stored in the freezer for a maximum of 30 days and thaw at room temperature. Use a microwave or a saucepan to reheat the spaghetti and sauce.

Nutrition: Calories: 215 Carbs: 44.4 g Fat: 1.9 g Protein: 18.1 g

14. Black Bean Quinoa Burgers

Preparation Time: 10 minutes

Cooking Time: 35 minutes

Servings: 4

Ingredients:

- 1 cup Quinoa (dry)

- 2 cups Black beans (cooked)

- ¼ cup Mexican chorizo seasoning

Directions:

1. Make sure to soak then cook ⅔ cup (113 g.) of dry black beans according to the procedure.

2. Make sure to preheat oven to 375°F/190°C and line a baking sheet with parchment paper.

3. Add cooked black beans, quinoa, and spices to the food processor. Blend until a chunky mixture, scraping down the sides of the food processor to prevent any lumps if necessary.

4. You can add ingredients to the bowl, then mash them until it turns into a chunky mixture.

5. Put every mixture on the baking sheet.

6. Make sure to flatten it into a 1-inch-thick square, then cut the square into 8 patties. Shape every in circles.

7. Bake patties for 10 minutes. Take the baking sheet off the oven, then flip the patties. Bake again for another 10 minutes.

8. Get the patties out once they are cooked. Make sure that crust is crispy and browned.

9. Let them cool down and enjoy!

Nutrition: Calories: 282 Carbs: 47.4 g. Fat: 3.4 g. Protein: 14.4 g.

15. Tomato Curry Fritters

Preparation Time: 10 minutes

Cooking Time: 16 minutes

Servings: 6

Ingredients:

- 5 cups Chickpeas (cooked or canned)
- 2 sweet onions (diced)
- 12 sundried tomatoes
- 3 cloves Garlic (minced)
- ¼ cup Curry spices

Directions:

1. If you're using dry chickpeas, make sure to soak and cook 1½ cup (330 g.) of dry chickpeas according to the method.
2. Preheat oven to 375°F/190°C. Place parchment paper on a baking sheet.

3. Put the chickpeas, onion, sundried tomatoes, garlic, and spices to the food processor and process them until it turns chunky mixture.

4. Alternatively, mince the sundried tomatoes, mash them together with the chickpeas and other ingredients in a large bowl, and knead them into a chunky mixture.

5. Take a tablespoon of the chickpea mixture and knead into a 2-inch-thick (5cm) disc, then place on the baking sheet until you make 24 fritters.

6. Afterward, bake the fritters for eight minutes. Take the baking sheet off the oven, turn the fritters over and bake for another 8 minutes.

7. Take fritters out of the oven once cooked. Make sure it is brown and crispy. Let them cool down.

Nutrition: Calories: 173 Carbs: 22 g Fat: 4 g Protein: 13 g Fiber:9.3g Sugar: 9 g

CHAPTER 4:

VEGETABLES, SALADS AND SIDES RECIPES

16. Strawberry Blue Cheese Arugula Salad

Preparation Time: 10 minutes

Cooking Time: 0 minutes

Servings: 4

Ingredients:

- 3 tablespoons olive oil
- 2 tablespoons balsamic vinegar
- 1 tablespoon honey
- 6 ounces arugula

- 2 cups sliced strawberries

- ⅓ Cup crumbled blue cheese

- Pinch Salt and Black pepper

Directions:

1. In a bowl, mix oil, vinegar, and honey for about 30 seconds or until well blended. Set aside.

2. Put the arugula in a large bowl. Top with the strawberries. Add the dressing and toss well, so all the greens and strawberries are coated. You can use more or less dressing, depending on your taste.

3. Sprinkle the cheese on top.

4. Season with salt and pepper to taste.

5. Simple Swap: For a tangy variation, use feta or goat cheese instead of blue cheese.

Nutrition: Calories: 100 Carbs: 3g Fat: 9g Protein: 3g

17. Cucumber Hummus Wraps

Preparation Time: 10 minutes

Cooking Time: 0 minutes

Servings: 4

Ingredients:

- ½ cup hummus
- 4 thin flatbread wraps or large tortillas
- 1 small cucumber, ends trimmed, thinly sliced
- ⅓ Cup chopped olives
- ¼ cup crumbled feta cheese with Mediterranean herbs
- Optional: roasted red peppers, baby spinach, thinly sliced tomatoes

Directions:

1. Spread hummus on one side of each flatbread or tortilla.
2. Top each with equally divided amounts of cucumbers, olives, and cheese.
3. Add any optional ingredients desired before rolling.

4. Roll each flatbread or tortilla tightly, making sure to tuck in the sides.

5. Leftovers Prep Tip: These wraps are perfect to make for lunch the night before because the flavors will blend together better. Make the wraps, then tightly wrap in foil. Your lunch is now ready for the next day.

Nutrition: Calories: 149 Carbs: 20g Fat: 6g Protein: 5g

18. White Bean Salad

Preparation Time: 3 minutes

Cooking Time: 0 minutes

Servings: 2

Ingredients:

- 1 can white beans, small
- 2 handful lambs lettuce
- 1 tablespoon mustard
- 1 tablespoon agave syrup
- 1 tablespoon balsamic vinegar

What you'll need from the store cupboard

- 1 orange
- 2 tablespoons olive oil
- ½ tablespoon thyme
- 1 pinch salt

Directions:

1. Drain the white beans, then rinse them.

2. Wash the lettuce thoroughly.

3. Peel and slice the orange.

4. Mix all the ingredients in a bowl.

5. All done, your salad is now ready. Serve and enjoy.

Nutrition: Calories 360 Fat 15g Carbs 45g Protein 14g

19. Quick White Bean Salad

Preparation Time: 10 minutes

Cooking Time: 0 minutes

Servings: 4

Ingredients:

- 1 can white beans
- 1 red onion
- 1 bell pepper, red
- 1 handful parsley, fresh
- 1 handful cilantro, fresh

What you'll need from the store cupboard

- 4 tomatoes, sun-dried
- 3 tablespoons olive oil
- 1 tablespoon lemon juice
- Salt to taste
- Pepper to taste

Directions:

1. Drain the beans and rinse them.
2. Dice the onions.
3. Wash the pepper and slice it into small pieces.
4. Slice the sun-dried tomatoes into small strips.
5. Add all the five ingredients with tomatoes into a bowl.
6. Add olive oil, lemon juice, then season with salt and pepper.
7. Serve with whole wheat bread if you desire.

Nutrition: Calories 389 Fat 22g Carbs 40g Protein 12g

20. Easy Green Bean Salad

Preparation Time: 10 minutes

Cooking Time: 0 minutes

Servings: 4

Ingredients:

- 1 jar green beans, medium
- 2 tablespoons vinegar
- 1 tablespoons sugar
- 1 handful parsley
- 1 red onion

What you'll need from the store cupboard

- 3 tablespoons olive oil
- ½ tablespoons salt
- ½ tablespoons pepper

Directions:

1. Drain the green beans and save the drained water.

2. Thinly slice the onion, then put it in a large bowl. Add the drained beans to the bowl.

3. Chop parsley and add it along with other ingredients in the bowl.

4. Mix the ingredients, then let rest for two to three hours.

5. Serve and enjoy.

Nutrition: Calories 254 Fat 21g Carbs 15g Protein 2g

21. Supercharging Avocado Chickpea Salad

Preparation Time: 5 minutes

Cooking Time: 0 minutes

Servings: 2

Ingredients:

- 1 can chickpeas
- 2 avocados
- 1 handful cilantro
- ½ red onion
- ½ cup feta cheese

What you'll need from the store cupboard

- 1 lime juice
- Salt to taste
- Pepper to taste

Directions:

1. Drain the chickpeas and rinse them.

2. Dice the avocados and chop the cilantro.

3. Dice the onion, then throw the chickpeas, cilantro, and onion in a large bowl.

4. Add cheese and lime juice to the bowl.

5. Season with salt and pepper to taste, then mix the ingredients. Serve and enjoy.

Nutrition: Calories 708 Fat 46g Carbs 57g Protein 19g

22. Watermelon Salad

Preparation Time: 5 minutes

Cooking Time: 0 minutes

Servings: 3

Ingredients:

- 3 cups cubed melon
- 3 tablespoons rice vinegar
- 1 tablespoon fresh basil, sliced thinly
- 1 tablespoon fresh mint, chopped
- 1 tablespoon fresh cilantro, chopped

What you'll need from the store cupboard

- Sea salt to taste

Directions:

1. Place the watermelon in a colander, then sprinkle salt as you toss the watermelon.
2. Let it rest so that some liquid will drain out.

3. Toss the watermelon with rice vinegar; 1 tablespoon of vinegar per one cup of melon.

4. Add herbs and mix well.

5. Serve and enjoy it when cold.

Nutrition: Calories 48 Fat 0g Carbs 12g Protein 1g

23. Vegetable Fried Brown Rice

Preparation Time: 5 minutes

Cooking Time: 15 minutes

Servings: 4

Ingredients:

- 1 cup mixed vegetables (frozen)
- 2 cups brown rice (cooked)
- 2 lightly whisked eggs
- ¼ - ⅓ cup of soy sauce (low-sodium)

What you'll need from store cupboard

- 1 tablespoon coconut oil
- Salt to taste
- Fresh ground pepper to taste

Directions:

1. Heat oil in a frying pan (large) over medium-high heat.
2. Add mixed vegetables, then cook for about 2 minutes while stirring.

3. Add rice and soy sauce. Cook for 5 minutes until heated through.

4. Make a well in the mixture center, then add eggs to the frying pan.

5. Let eggs cook for 1 minute. Use a spoon to break them up into small pieces.

6. Season with additional soy sauce, pepper, and salt to taste.

7. Serve with sriracha and enjoy.

Nutrition: Calories: 279 Fat: 8g Carbs: 45.8g Protein: 10.5g

CHAPTER 5:

DESSERT RECIPES

24. Chocolate-Peppermint Nice Cream

Preparation Time: 30 minutes

Cooking Time: 0 minutes

Servings: 2

Ingredients:

- 3 frozen ripe bananas, broken into thirds
- 3 tablespoons plant-based milk (here or here)
- 2 tablespoons cocoa powder
- ⅛ Teaspoon peppermint extract

Directions:

1. Combine the bananas, milk, cocoa powder, and peppermint in a food processor.

2. Process on medium speed for 30 to 60 seconds, or until the bananas have been blended into smooth soft-serve consistency, and serve.

Nutrition: Calories: 173 Total fat: 2g Carbohydrates: 43g Fiber: 6g Protein: 3g

25. Strawberry-Watermelon Ice Pops

Preparation Time: 5 minutes

Cooking Time: 0 minutes

Servings: 6

Ingredients:

- 4 cups diced watermelon
- 4 strawberries, tops removed
- 2 tablespoons freshly squeezed lime juice

Directions:

1. Combine the watermelon, strawberries, and lime juice In a blender. Blend for 1 to 2 minutes, or until well combined.

2. Pour into 6 ice-pop molds evenly, then insert ice-pop sticks. Freeze for at least 6 hours before serving.

Nutrition: Calories: 61 Total fat: 0g Carbohydrates: 15g Fiber: 1g Protein: 1g

26. Oat Crunch Apple Crisp

Preparation Time: 10 minutes

Cooking Time: 35 minutes

Servings: 6

Ingredients:

- 3 medium apples, cored and cut into ¼-inch pieces
- ¾ cup apple juice
- 1 teaspoon vanilla extract
- 1 teaspoon ground cinnamon, divided
- 2 cups rolled oats
- ¼ cup maple syrup

Directions:

1. Preheat the oven to 375°F.
2. Combine the apple slices, apple juice, vanilla, and ½ teaspoon of cinnamon in a large bowl. Mix well to thoroughly coat the apple slices.

3. Layer apple slices on the bottom of a round or square baking dish. Take any leftover liquid and pour it over the apple slices.

4. Stir together the oats, maple syrup, and the remaining ½ teaspoon of cinnamon until the oats are completely coated in a large bowl.

5. Sprinkle the oat mixture over the apples, being sure to spread it out evenly so that none of the apple slices are visible.

6. Set 35 minutes to bake or until the oats begin to turn golden brown and serve.

Nutrition: Calories: 213 Total fat: 2g Carbohydrates: 47g Fiber: 6g Protein: 4g

CHAPTER 6:

SNACK RECIPES

27. Teriyaki Tempeh and Broccoli

Preparation Time: 10 minutes

Cooking Time: 10 minutes

Servings: 2

Ingredients:

- ¼ cup tamari or soy sauce
- ¼ cup water
- 1 tablespoon olive oil
- 1 tablespoon pure maple syrup or unrefined sugar
- 1 teaspoon cornstarch or arrowroot powder
- ½ teaspoon ground ginger
- Fresh ginger
- 1 (8- or 9-ounce) tempeh, cubed
- ½ head broccoli, cut into pieces

Directions:

1. Mix the tamari, water, olive oil, maple syrup, cornstarch, and ginger in a pressure cooker. Add the tempeh. Close and lock the lid, then ensure the pressure valve is sealed. Select high pressure and set for 5 minutes.

2. When cooking is complete, quick release the pressure, being careful not to get your fingers or face near the steam release.

3. Once pressure is released, carefully unlock the lid and mix.

4. Serving tip: For a complete meal, serve this dish with cooked quinoa or Cilantro-Lime Brown and Wild Rice, sprinkled with toasted sesame seeds or cashews. Try garnishing the dish with sliced scallions.

Nutrition: Calories: 336 Total fat: 18g Protein: 25g Sodium: 2g Fiber: 3g

28. Peach Crisp

Preparation Time: 15 minutes

Cooking Time: 2 hours

Servings: 5

Ingredients:

- 3 large peaches, peeled, pitted, and sliced
- ⅓ Cup all-purpose flour
- ⅓ Cup quick-cooking oats
- ⅓ Cup brown sugar
- ½ teaspoon ground cinnamon
- ⅛ Teaspoon ground nutmeg
- 4 tablespoons (½ stick) unsalted butter
- Vanilla ice cream, for serving

Directions:

1. Put the peaches in the slow cooker.

2. Mix the flour, oats, brown sugar, cinnamon, and nutmeg in a bowl. Using the pastry blender, make the butter into the flour mixture until it is crumbly. Sprinkle the mixture over the peaches.

3. Double layer paper towels on top of the slow cooker and secure with the lid. Cook on high for 2 hours.

4. Serve with your favorite vanilla ice cream.

Nutrition: Calories: 207 Total Fat: 10g Cholesterol: 24mg Carbohydrates: 28g Fiber: 2g Protein: 3g

29. Banana Bread

Preparation Time: 15 minutes

Cooking Time: 2 hours and 30 minutes

Servings: 8

Ingredients:

- ⅓ Cup milk
- 3 tablespoons canola oil
- 1 large egg, lightly beaten
- 3 medium ripe bananas, mashed
- 2½ cups all-purpose flour
- ½ cup granulated sugar
- ½ cup brown sugar
- 3½ teaspoons baking powder
- 1 teaspoon salt

Directions:

1. Whisk milk, oil, egg, and mashed bananas together in a bowl. Add the flour, granulated sugar, brown sugar, baking powder, and salt. Mix it until no flour streaks remain.

2. Grease a loaf pan that will fit inside your slow cooker insert. Pour the butter into the loaf pan.

3. Put the trivet in a slow cooker. Place the loaf pan on the trivet. Double layer paper towels on top of the slow cooker and secure with the lid. Cook on high for 2½ hours.

4. Take the loaf pan from the slow cooker and let it sit for 15 minutes. Slice and serve warm.

Nutrition: Calories: 333 Total Fat: 7g Cholesterol: 24mg Carbohydrates: 66g Fiber: 2g Protein: 6g

30. Mexican Beans and Rice

Preparation Time: 5 minutes

Cooking Time: 3 hours

Servings: 4

Ingredients:

- 1 (15-ounce) can black beans
- ¾ cup long-grain brown rice
- 1½ cups water
- ¾ cup salsa
- 1 bay leaf
- 1 teaspoon ground cumin
- ½ teaspoon garlic powder
- ½ teaspoon salt
- 1 to 2 tablespoons fresh lime juice
- Sour cream, for topping (optional)

Directions:

1. Combine the beans, rice, water, salsa, bay leaf, cumin, garlic powder, and salt in the slow cooker.

2. Cook on low for 3 hours.

3. Discard the bay leaf. Add the lime juice and additional salsa, if desired.

4. Serve it a dollop of sour cream.

Nutrition: Calories: 262 Total Fat: 2g Cholesterol: 0mg Sodium: 587mg Carbohydrates: 52g Fiber: 10g Protein: 11g

31. Spaghetti Squash with Feta

Preparation Time: 5 minutes

Cooking Time: 6 hours

Servings: 2

Ingredients:

- 1 small (1- to 2-pound) spaghetti squash
- 1 cup water
- ¼ cup heavy cream
- 3 garlic cloves, minced
- 3 tablespoons unsalted butter
- ½ cup feta cheese
- Salt
- Freshly ground black pepper
- 2 tablespoons chopped fresh parsley, for garnish

Directions:

1. Cut 6 to 8 slits all over the spaghetti squash. Place the squash in the slow cooker. Add the water.

2. Cook on low for 6 hours.

3. Transfer squash to the cutting board and allow it to cool slightly. Once you can handle it, slice the squash lengthwise and remove the seeds. Scrape the flesh to create long strands resembling spaghetti using a fork.

4. Return the squash strands to the slow cooker and turn to low. Add the cream, garlic, and butter and stir gently to combine. Add the feta. Season with salt and pepper. Garnish with chopped parsley and serve.

Nutrition: Calories: 453 Total Fat: 34g Cholesterol: 100mg; Sodium: 705mg Carbohydrates: 35g Fiber: 0g Protein: 9g

32. Zucchini Noodles with Marinara Sauce

Preparation Time: 15 minutes

Cooking Time: 8 hours

Servings: 6

Ingredients:

- 2 (28-ounce) cans crushed tomatoes
- 1 can diced tomatoes
- Green peppers
- Onion
- 1 (6-ounce) can tomato paste
- 1 bay leaf
- 2 teaspoons dried basil
- 1 teaspoon garlic powder
- ½ teaspoon dried oregano
- 1 teaspoon brown sugar
- 2 tablespoons olive oil

- Salt

- Freshly ground black pepper

- 4 medium zucchini, trimmed

Directions:

1. Combine the crushed tomatoes, diced tomatoes with their juice, tomato paste, bay leaf, basil, garlic powder, oregano, and brown sugar in the slow cooker. Stir to combine.

2. Cook on low for 8 hours.

3. Discard the bay leaf. Stir in the olive oil. Season with salt and pepper.

4. Using a spiralizer, make zucchini noodles. Place zucchini noodles in the microwave-safe dish. Set it on high for 3 minutes. Pile the zucchini on individual serving plates and top with marinara sauce.

Nutrition: Calories: 156 Total Fat: 5g Cholesterol: 0mg Sodium: 422mg Carbohydrates: 24g Fiber: 8g Protein: 7g

33. Coconut Curry with Vegetables

Preparation Time: 5 minutes

Cooking Time: 4 hours

Servings: 4

Ingredients:

- 1 (13.5-ounce) can coconut milk, stirred
- 2 tablespoons red curry paste
- 2 tablespoons instant tapioca
- 1 (1-pound) package frozen stir-fry vegetables
- 1 (15-ounce) can chickpeas, rinsed and drained
- Salt
- Freshly ground black pepper

Directions:

1. Combine the coconut milk, curry paste, and tapioca in the slow cooker. Stir until the curry paste is thoroughly blended into the milk. Stir in the vegetables and chickpeas.
2. Cook on low for 4 hours.

3. Season with salt and pepper and serve.

Nutrition: Calories: 483 Total Fat: 28g Saturated Fat: 23g Sodium: 780mg Carbohydrates: 50g Fiber: 11g Protein: 10g

CHAPTER 7:

JUICES AND SMOOTHIES RECIPES

34. Endless Energy Smoothie

Preparation Time: 3 minutes

Cooking Time: 0 minutes

Servings: 2

Ingredients:

- 1 frozen banana, chopped
- 11/2 cup green tea
- 1 cup chopped pineapple
- 1 lime, juiced

- 1 tbsp. chia seeds

Directions:

1. Combine all ingredients in a high-speed blender and blend until smooth.

Nutrition: Calories: 49 Carbohydrates: 11g Total fat: 0g Protein: 0g

35. High-fibre Fruit Smoothie

Preparation Time: 3 minutes

Cooking Time: 0 minutes

Servings: 2

Ingredients:

- 1 frozen banana, chopped
- 1 cup orange juice
- 2 cups chopped papaya
- 1 cup shredded cabbage
- 1 tbsp. chia seeds

Directions:

1. Combine all ingredients in a high-speed blender and blend until smooth.

Nutrition: Calories: 168 Carbohydrates: 26g Total fat: 3g Protein: 6g

36. Nutritious Green Smoothie

Preparation Time: 3 minutes

Cooking Time: 0 minutes

Servings: 2

Ingredients:

- 2-3 frozen broccoli florets
- 1 cup apple juice
- 1 large pear, chopped
- 1 kiwi, peeled and chopped
- 1 cup spinach leaves

Directions:

1. Combine all ingredients in a high-speed blender and blend until smooth.

Nutrition: Calories: 44 Carbohydrates: 0g Total fat: 0g Protein: 0g

37. Apricot, Strawberry, and Banana Smoothie

Preparation Time: 3 minutes

Cooking Time: 0 minutes

Servings: 2

Ingredients:

- 1 frozen banana
- 1 1/2 cup almond milk
- 5 dried apricots
- 1 cup fresh strawberries

Directions:

1. Combine all ingredients in a high-speed blender and blend until smooth.

Nutrition: Calories: 69 Carbohydrates: 17g Total fat: 0g Protein: 1g

38. Spinach and Green Apple Smoothie

Preparation Time: 3 minutes

Cooking Time: 0 minutes

Servings: 2

Ingredients:

- 3-4 ice cubes
- 1 cup unsweetened almond milk
- 1 banana, peeled and chopped
- 2 green apples, peeled and chopped
- 1 cup raw spinach leaves
- 3-4 dates, pitted

Directions:

1. Combine all ingredients in a high-speed blender and blend until smooth.

Nutrition: Calories: 249 Carbohydrates: 46g Total fat: 3g Protein: 9g

39. Super food Blueberry Smoothie

Preparation Time: 3 minutes

Cooking Time: 0 minutes

Servings: 2

Ingredients:

- 2-3 cubes frozen spinach
- 1 cup green tea
- 1 banana
- 2 cups blueberries
- 1 tbsp. ground flaxseed

Directions:

1. Combine all ingredients in a high-speed blender and blend until smooth.

Nutrition: Calories: 249 Carbohydrates: 46g Total fat: 3g Protein: 9g

CHAPTER 8:

OTHER RECIPES

40. Squash Lentil Soup

Preparation Time: 10 Minutes

Cooking Time: 35 Minutes

Servings: 4

Ingredients:

- 7 cups Vegetable Broth
- 2 tbsp. Olive Oil
- 2 tsp., Sage dried
- 1 Yellow Onion, medium & diced.
- Salt & Pepper to taste
- 1 Butternut Squash
- 1 ½ cup Red Lentils

Directions:

1. Using a saucepan, start heating your oil and stir in the onions.
2. Sauté the onions for 2 to 3 minutes or until softened.
3. Once cooked, stir in squash and sage while stirring continuously.

4. Then, spoon in the lentils, salt, and pepper.

5. Bring the lentil mixture to a boil for about 30 minutes. Lower the heat.

6. Then, allow the soup to cool down until the lentils are soft.

7. Finally, transfer the mixture to a high-speed blender and blend for 3 to 4 minutes or until smooth.

8. Serve hot.

Nutrition: Calories: 421 Kcal Protein: 16.7g Carbohydrates: 51g Fat: 4.5g

41. Sweet Potato Gnocchi

Preparation Time: 30 minutes

Cooking Time: 30 minutes

Servings: 2

Ingredients

- 2 cups flour

- ¼ teaspoon salt

- ½ teaspoon turmeric

- 3 garlic cloves, roasted

- 1 sweet potato

Directions

1. To begin this recipe, you will want to heat your oven to 375°f. Once the oven is warm, place the sweet potato on a baking sheet and pop it in for thirty minutes.

2. During the last five minutes of the bake time, add the garlic cloves into the oven and allow them to roast.

3. When the time is up, remove the baking sheet from the oven and allow the ingredients to cool for ten minutes or so.

4. Next, you will want to remove the skin of the sweet potato. Once this is done, place the sweet potato into a mixing bowl and add in the garlic. Carefully take a fork and mash everything together until there are no chunks.

5. At this point, you can season the sweet potato with turmeric and salt.

6. With the sweet potato now seasoned, it is time to add the flour. You will want to add the flour in half of a cup at a time.

7. Be sure to stir the ingredients together well before you add any more flour. The amount of flour may vary depending on the size of the sweet potato. You will want to continue adding flour until it becomes difficult to stir.

8. Now, your sweet potato should have a dough-like consistency. Break the dough up and roll the sweet potato into strips.

9. Using a knife, you can cut these strips into half-inch pieces.

10. Once you have finished making your gnocchi, you will want to take a large pot of water and bring it to a boil over high heat.

11. When your water is boiling carefully drop in the gnocchi pieces.

12. When they are cooked through, the pieces will rise to the top. Typically, this will take two to three minutes. Enjoy!

Nutrition: Calories: 460 Fat: 5 g Carbs: 45 g Protein: 10 g

42. Taco Pasta Bowl

Preparation Time: 10 minutes

Cooking Time: 30 minutes

Servings: 4

Ingredients:

- 1 can black beans
- 1 cup corn
- ½ cup diced onion
- 1 jar salsa
- 1 box pasta
- ¼ teaspoon cumin
- 2 tablespoons chili powder

Directions:

1. To start, please cook the pasta of your choice according to the directions provided on the box. Once this step is complete, you can drain the water and set the pasta to the side.

2. Next, you will want to take a medium pan and place it over medium to high heat. Add one tablespoon of your oil and bring it to sizzle. Once the oil is hot, place your onion and cook for three to five minutes. By the end, the onion should be soft.

3. At this point, you will add in the beans, corn, salsa, and spices. I have chosen to use chili powder and cumin, but you can spice your dish however you would like!

4. Last, you will pour your sauce over your pasta and enjoy!

Nutrition: Calories: 480 Fat: 8 g Carbs: 46 g Protein: 18 g

43. Vegan BBQ Tofu

Preparation Time: 10 minutes

Cooking Time: 40 minutes

Servings: 3

Ingredients:

- ¼ cup vegan BBQ sauce
- ¼ teaspoon pepper
- ¼ teaspoon garlic powder
- ¼ teaspoon salt
- 1 tablespoon grapeseed oil
- 1 pack firm tofu

Directions:

1. Before you begin cooking your tofu, you will want to press it. Generally, this will take thirty to forty-five minutes. If possible, try to press the tofu overnight so that it is ready for you when you need it.

2. Once your tofu is ready, bring a saucepan over medium heat and allow it to warm up. As your saucepan is warming up, slice your tofu into small pieces. Put a 1 tablespoon of oil and spread your tofu across the pan. At this point, season your tofu and cook for five minutes. Be sure to flip each piece of tofu until it is a nice golden-brown color all over.

3. Finally, remove the tofu from the pan and cover it in BBQ sauce. This meal is excellent alone or with your favorite grain or vegetable.

Nutrition: Calories: 290, Fat: 64 g, Carbs: 25 g, Protein: 20 g

44. Mustard Tomato Mix

Preparation time: 10 minutes

Cooking time: 10 minutes

Servings: 4

Ingredients:

- 2 pounds plum tomatoes, sliced
- A pinch of salt and black pepper
- 2 tablespoons avocado oil
- 3 tablespoons lime juice
- 1 tablespoon Dijon mustard
- 1 tablespoon mint, chopped

Directions:

1. Using a pan, heat your oil over medium heat, add the tomatoes, the lime juice, and the other ingredients, toss, cook for 10 minutes, divide between plates and serve.

Nutrition: Calories: 120 Fat: 4 g Carbs: 15 g Protein: 6 g

45. Veggies and noodle bowl with mushrooms

Preparation Time: 10 minutes

Cooking Time: 20 minutes

Servings: 2

Ingredients:

- 8 ounces sliced mushrooms
- 9 oz. rinsed and sliced leeks
- 8 ounces noodles
- 5 ounces baby spinach

Directions:

1. Boil the noodles according to the given directions on the packet, remove the boiling water, rinse with cold water, and set aside.
2. Now take a bowl, add all the ingredients, and whisk them well until all the ingredients are combined well.

Nutrition: Calories: 260 Fat: 4 g Carbs: 35 g Protein: 4 g

46. Broccoli over Orzo

Preparation Time: 10 minutes

Cooking Time: 25 minutes

Servings: 3

Ingredients:

- 3 teaspoons olive oil
- 4 garlic cloves, smashed
- 2 cups broccoli florets
- 4½ ounces orzo pasta
- ¼ teaspoon salt
- ¼ teaspoon pepper

Directions:

1. Start off by preparing your broccoli. You can do this by trimming the stems off and slicing the broccoli into small, bite-size pieces. If you want, go ahead and season with salt.

2. Next, you will want to steam your broccoli over a little bit of water until it is cooked through. Once the broccoli is cooked, chop it up into even smaller pieces.

3. When the broccoli is done, cook your pasta according to the directions provided on the box. Once this is done, drain the water and then place the pasta back into the pot.

4. With the pasta and broccoli done, place it back into the pot with the garlic. Stir everything together well and cook until the garlic turns a nice golden color. Be sure to stir everything to combine your meal well. Serve warm and enjoy a simple dinner!

Nutrition: Calories: 310 Fat: 4 g Carbs: 35 g Protein: 10 g

47. Mango Pineapple Hoisin Sauce

Preparation Time: 10 minutes

Cooking Time: 10 minutes

Servings: 2

Ingredients:

- 1 ½ cups fresh mango juice or pureed mango
- ⅔ cup vegan hoisin sauce
- 4 tablespoons brown rice vinegar
- 1 cup fresh pineapple juice
- ½ cup tamari or soy sauce
- 2 tablespoons Sriracha sauce

Directions:

1. Use a pan and heat oil over medium heat.
2. Add all the ingredients and stir constantly.
3. Simmer until the mixture thickens.

Nutrition: Calories: 125 Fat: 2 g Carbs: 8 g Protein: 4.3 g

48. Sriracha Sauce

Preparation Time: 20 minutes

Cooking Time: 10 minutes

Servings: 2

Ingredients

- 15 red Fresno chilies, chopped into chunks
- ½ tablespoon salt
- 4 garlic cloves
- ¼ cup apple cider or white vinegar
- 2 tablespoons raw sugar

Directions:

1. Place the chilies, garlic, salt, and sugar into a food processor. Pulse until coarsely chopped. Transfer into a mason's jar.
2. Cover with a plastic cling and leave it for 5-7 days to ferment. Stir often during this period. In 3-4 days you will see some bubbles appearing.

3. Transfer the contents of the jar into a blender. Add vinegar and blend until smooth.

4. Transfer into a saucepan after passing through a wire mesh strainer.

5. Bring to a boil on high heat.

6. When it starts boiling, reduce the heat and simmer for 5 minutes. Remove from heat and cool.

7. Transfer into a flip top bottle. Refrigerate until use.

Nutrition: Calories: 90 Fat: 6 g Carbs: 5 g Protein: 1 g

49. White Sauce (Béchamel)

Preparation Time: 10 minutes

Cooking Time: 12 minutes

Servings: 2

Ingredients:

- 6 tablespoons olive oil
- 4 cups soymilk or any other non-dairy milk of your choice
- 5 tablespoons all-purpose flour
- Sea salt to taste
- Black pepper to taste

Directions:

1. Place a heavy pot over a medium heat. Add oil. When the oil is heated, add sifted flour into the pan. Stir constantly for about a minute. It will begin to change color; be careful not to burn it!
2. Pour in the milk, stirring constantly. Keep stirring until thick.
3. Simmer until the thickness you desire is nearly achieved. This is because the sauce thickens further as it cools.

4. Turn off the heat. Add salt, pepper, and any other herbs and spices if you desire.

Nutrition: Calories: 68 Fat: 2 g Carbs: 1.5 g Protein: 5 g

50. Butter Bean Hummus

Preparation Time 5 Minutes

Cook Time: 0 Minutes

Servings: 4

Ingredients:

- 1 can butter beans, drained, rinsed
- 2 garlic cloves, minced
- ½ lemon, juiced
- 1 Tbsps. olive oil
- 4 sprigs of parsley, minced
- ¼ tsp. Sea salt

Directions:

1. Blend all ingredients in a food processor into a creamy mixture.
2. Serve as a dip for bread, crackers, or any type of vegetables.

Nutrition: Calories 84 Fat 3.9g Carbohydrate 10.2g Protein 3.1g

CONCLUSION

Well done! Thank you for reaching the end of this book, The Complete Vegetarian Cookbook.

Hopefully, this book has helped you understand that making vegetarian recipes and diet easier can improve your life, not only by improving your health and helping you lose weight, but also by saving you money and time.

Remember that vegetarianism is a choice, not a religion.

Be flexible when it comes to your diet and enjoy new tastes and experiences.

Don't be afraid of meat substitutes, but experiment with using them sparingly. There is no need to completely replace meat with fake meat products like tofu or processed soy-based vegetarian burgers and hot dogs. Not only are they expensive, but fake meats contain artificial ingredients that may or may not be healthy for you.

Also, if you are not used to eating a vegetarian diet, start with a few vegetarian meals and snacks during the week, and see how you feel.

You can always add more vegetarian meals to your diet later. It is better to be even slightly vegetarians than completely non-vegetarian.

The best tip I can give you about making vegetarian recipes is to experiment and have fun!

Here are some more tips to help you with your vegetarian diet:

1. Remember that vegetarianism is not a destination, it is a journey.

2. A vegetarian diet is plant-based. This means that you should try to eat more plants and less animal products. You should also be careful not to replace whole foods with their processed counterparts, such as replacing whole foods such as fruits and vegetables with fruit juice and pasta sauce.

3. Try to avoid processed food whenever possible, while still maintaining your balanced diet and nutrients that you need for your health. An easier way of doing this will be to make your own food when

possible and try to avoid packaged, pre-prepared foods at the grocery store.

4. Avoid processed food products that contain artificial ingredients, such as sweeteners, colors, and flavors.

5. Avoid highly processed meat substitutes. Remember to use meat substitutes in moderation or as an occasional treat.

6. If you choose to eat meat substitutes such as tofu, be sure to thoroughly cook it and try different ways of preparing it

7. You may need to gradually introduce your family and friends to your new eating habits. Don't expect everyone to support you or enjoy the same things you do when it comes to vegetarian recipes. As long as you are happy with your food choices, that is the most important thing – even if it means making some changes at home!

When you are having a hard time, always remember this: You can always choose to stop being a vegetarian.

You can simply start eating meat again if you are struggling with your new diet.

Remember that it is okay to be a part-time vegetarian, but if you find that you cannot maintain the lifestyle or are unhappy with your choice, it is always better to go back to eating a non-veg diet.

There is no shame in making changes to your vegetarian recipe routine if you need to, and you will not shame yourself for deciding that a strict vegetarian diet does not work for you.

I know that there are many books and choosing my book is amazing. I am thankful that you stopped and took the time to decide. You made a great decision, and I am sure that you enjoyed it.

I will be even happier if you will add some comments. Feedbacks helped by growing, and they still do. They help me to choose better content and new ideas. So, maybe your feedback can trigger an idea for my next book. Thank you again for downloading this book!

I hope you enjoyed reading my book!

www.ingramcontent.com/pod-product-compliance
Lightning Source LLC
Chambersburg PA
CBHW070933080526
44589CB00013B/1504